ROBERT HOLMAN

Robert Holman was born in 1952 and brought up on a farm in North Yorkshire. He was awarded an Arts Council Writers' Bursary in 1974, and since then he has spent periods as resident dramatist with the Royal National Theatre and with the Royal Shakespeare Company in Stratford-upon-Avon. He has written extensively for both theatre and television, and his stage plays, including *Outside the Whale*, *German Skerries*, for which he won the George Devine Award, *Other Worlds*, *Today*, *Making Noise Quietly*, *Across Oka*, *Rafts and Dreams* and *Bad Weather* have been seen in cities as far apart as Los Angeles and Tokyo, following their premieres at such theatres as the Royal Court, the RSC, the Bush and the Edinburgh Traverse. His first novel, *The Amish Landscape*, was published in 1992.

Other titles in this series

Caryl Churchill
BLUE HEART
CHURCHILL PLAYS: THREE
CHURCHILL: SHORTS
CLOUD NINE
HOTEL
ICECREAM
LIGHT SHINING IN
  BUCKINGHAMSHIRE
MAD FOREST
THE SKRIKER
THIS IS A CHAIR
TRAPS

John Clifford
LIGHT IN THE VILLAGE

Ariel Dorfman
DEATH AND THE MAIDEN
READER
WIDOWS
THE RESISTANCE TRILOGY

David Edgar
DR JEKYLL AND MR HYDE
EDGAR: SHORTS
PENTECOST
THE SHAPE OF THE TABLE

Helen Edmundson
ANNA KARENINA
THE CLEARING
THE MILL ON THE FLOSS
WAR AND PEACE

Kevin Elyot
THE DAY I STOOD STILL
MY NIGHT WITH REG

Peter Flannery
SINGER

Pam Gems
DEBORAH'S DAUGHTER
STANLEY

Robert Holman
BAD WEATHER

Tony Kushner
ANGELS IN AMERICA
Parts One and Two

Stephen Jeffreys
THE CLINK
A GOING CONCERN
THE LIBERTINE

Larry Kramer
THE DESTINY OF ME
THE NORMAL HEART

Mike Leigh
ECSTASY
SMELLING A RAT

Clare McIntyre
MY HEART'S A SUITCASE
  & LOW LEVEL PANIC

Conor McPherson
FOUR PLAYS
THE WEIR

Terence Rattigan
AFTER THE DANCE
THE BROWNING VERSION
THE DEEP BLUE SEA
FRENCH WITHOUT TEARS
SEPARATE TABLES
THE WINSLOW BOY

ROBERT HOLMAN

Making Noise Quietly

three short plays

Being Friends
Lost
Making Noise Quietly

NICK HERN BOOKS
LONDON

A Nick Hern Book

Making Noise Quietly, consisting of *Being Friends*, *Lost* and *Making Noise Quietly*, published in this edition in 1999 as an original paperback by Nick Hern Books Limited, 14 Larden Road, London W3 7ST

First published by Methuen London Limited in 1987

Making Noise Quietly copyright © 1987 Robert Holman

Robert Holman has asserted his moral right to be identified as the author of this work

Cover image: Oxford Stage Company's production of *Making Noise Quietly*. Illustration by Andrew Williamson

Typeset by Country Setting, Kingsdown, Kent CT14 8ES
Printed in England by Athenaeum Press Ltd,
Gateshead, Tyne and Wear NE11 0PZ

ISBN 1-845459-452-4

A CIP catalogue record for this book is available from the British Library

To Chris Pratt

Being Friends, *Lost* and *Making Noise Quietly* were performed
as a trilogy under the collective title *Making Noise Quietly*
at the Bush Theatre, London, on 26 June 1986, with the
following cast:

One
Being Friends

OLIVER BELL	Jonathan Cullen
ERIC FABER	Ronan Vibert

Two
Lost

MAY APPLETON	Jean Boht
GEOFFREY CHURCH	Jonathan Coy

Three
Making Noise Quietly

HELENE ENSSLIN	Helen Ryan
ALAN TADD	Paul Copley
SAM	Daniel Kipling

Directed by John Dove
Designed by Kenny Miller
Lighting by Paul Denby

The trilogy, *Making Noise Quietly*, was revived by the Oxford Stage Company at the Whitehall Theatre, London, on 14 April 1999. Press night was 19 April. The company had already toured the production to Oxford, Cambridge, Manchester and Edinburgh. The cast was as follows:

One
Being Friends

OLIVER BELL	John Lloyd Fillingham
ERIC FABER	Peter Hanly

Two
Lost

MAY APPLETON	Eleanor Bron
GEOFFREY CHURCH	Peter Hanly

Three
Making Noise Quietly

HELENE ENSSLIN	Eleanor Bron
ALAN TADD	John Lloyd Fillingham
SAM	Phillip Dowling

Directed by Deborah Bruce
Designed by Anthony MacIlwaine
Lighting by Michael Hulls
Produced by Dominic Dromgoole

One

BEING FRIENDS

Characters

OLIVER BELL, *the farmer*
ERIC FABER, *the artist*

The corner of a field at Oxen Hoath in Kent. July 1944.

The corner of a field close to the pond at Oxen Hoath in Kent. July 1944.

It is a pasture field, the grass rough and undulating.

OLIVER BELL *is lying sunbathing.*

OLIVER *is a robust and strong young man of twenty-five. His features have a clean and refined look. He is wearing very baggy working trousers with the braces off and hanging loosely from the waist. The rest of his clothes, including his shoes and socks, are scattered to one side.*

ERIC FABER *enters, riding on the pedal of his bicycle.*

ERIC *is a small and thin young man of twenty-three. He is frail, but his features are sharp. He is neatly dressed and has a short-sleeved jersey over his shirt. He has wire-framed glasses and there is a school-type satchel on his back.*

OLIVER *sits up as* ERIC *enters.* ERIC *steps off the pedal and the bicycle comes to a halt.*

ERIC. I like to come here at least once every fortnight. It's my favourite picnicking place. How long have you been here?

OLIVER. About an hour.

ERIC. I stopped off at Hadlow and looked at the church. Then I came away because the vicar disturbed me. I had planned to sketch one of the porticos. Have you been swimming in the pond?

OLIVER. I wasn't sure you could.

ERIC. A group of local boys have built a diving-board from the little bridge. With a plank and some rope, it's rather clever. Perhaps we could swim together, later?

OLIVER (*shyly*). Yes, all right.

ERIC. If the boys arrive we could join them. The vicar's a

terrible nuisance. I just get my pencils out when up he comes, wanting to know everything. I felt sad making my excuse and running, because I suspect he's rather lonely.

ERIC *unfastens the cane picnic hamper which is strapped to the back of his bicycle.*

I must look foolish dressed for cloudy.

ERIC *half stops, half lets the bicycle fall so that it lies on the grass. He struggles out of his satchel. He takes his glasses off and puts them on the hamper. He takes his jersey off. He puts his glasses back on.*

Where have you come from?

OLIVER. Erm, from a farm over there.

ERIC *looks.*

You can't see it – it's about a mile and a half through the trees.

ERIC *looks back to* OLIVER.

I was milking before I left. I didn't change.

ERIC. May I?

ERIC *leans forward, he sniffs* OLIVER*'s trouser legs.*

I get drunk on that smell.

ERIC *straightens up.*

OLIVER. I washed in the pond. For reasons I don't understand, I get Tuesday afternoon off. I'm beginning my fourth week here. Where d'you live?

ERIC. In Tonbridge.

OLIVER. With your family?

ERIC. Good heavens. No, I live with a friend of mine. And my housekeeper, Helen Nicholson. My friend is in London all this week.

ERIC *sits down a short distance from* OLIVER. *As he does so he winces very slightly.*

I had an accident. On my bicycle travelling to my aunt's in Greenwich, I was knocked over by a car. When I came to, it was like being in a cloud, with faces peering down. I realise now they were asking me how I felt, but just then I was too numb to know. At hospital they found, amongst other things, I'd a fractured spine.

OLIVER *pulls a face.*

I did give the nurses hell of course, for the nine months of my stay. Refusing this, refusing that. I was drunk on selfpity like a small child.

A slight pause.

I do suspect they want the child in you. It makes one manageable, especially when one is learning to walk again.

OLIVER. I'm sorry. I hope you're better.

ERIC. Oh much. I screamed and screamed like Violet Elizabeth. And you?

OLIVER. I'm a conscientious objector. I come from a Quaker family in Manchester.

ERIC. I don't know that part of the world. I've walked in the south, mainly through Suffolk.

OLIVER (*shrugging*). I don't know the south.

ERIC. If I have to spend a day in bed I like reading Ordnance maps.

A slight pause.

I've bread and cheese if you'd care to share it?

OLIVER (*shyly*). Thank you.

ERIC. I brought only enough for one. We'll have to behave like the five thousand.

OLIVER *smiles.*

ERIC *takes and opens the hamper.*

I've beer and a few cherries, too.

He takes a bottle of beer. He gives it to OLIVER.

OLIVER. Thank you.

    ERIC *takes another bottle. They open them and drink.*

    I see now why you had your accident.

ERIC. I am not irresponsible. It was a lady driver, her brakes had failed. I didn't see her coming towards the crossroads.

    ERIC *takes a small white linen cloth from the hamper; he spreads it on the grass.*

    You are correct though. I do love recklessness.

OLIVER. I suppose I tend to be a bit more careful.

ERIC. I must live a more trivial life than you.

    ERIC *takes the bread and cheese from the hamper and puts it onto the white cloth. They look at it. It doesn't look very much.*

    ERIC *takes the brown paper bag of cherries from the hamper. He puts the bag on the cloth and tears down the side so that the cherries fall out.*

    They look at it.

OLIVER. Shall I?

    OLIVER *breaks the bread in half.* ERIC *breaks the cheese. They begin to eat.*

ERIC. The bread is freshly baked by a friend of mine.

OLIVER. Who's that?

ERIC. She's a semi-successful painter called Beatrice Sloman. In London she's known at the more obscure galleries. Her work's becoming fashionable. She lives in Tonbridge. I rent my cottage from her. She's a lesbian. I like that kind of lady.

OLIVER. Tell her she bakes lovely bread.

ERIC. I shall tell her I met a beautiful young man lying in the grass.

A slight pause.

OLIVER. That's an exaggeration.

ERIC. But you are beautiful.

A slight pause.

Have you met many people, or made many friends?

OLIVER. No, not really. Mr and Mrs Whittle, who own the farm, are very nice but not very good at conversation. I tend to stay in my room reading. They're elderly – she in her seventies. Mr Whittle is a gruff old man.

A slight pause.

I think they find a stranger difficult, yet they need me. It's a lot of work.

A slight pause.

Their only son died. Before the war. They've been struggling on ever since.

ERIC. How have they reacted to you?

OLIVER. I think the war passes them by. I've had more trouble in the village – I was spat at one night by a youth. The barman made a snide joke to someone else. One woman won't serve me in her shop.

A slight pause.

In Manchester a whole street wouldn't talk to me. By comparison it's nothing.

A slight pause.

I know I'm not the coward they presume. What is it that you do?

ERIC. At the moment I'm involved in a series of sketches for *Vogue* magazine, illustrating the signs of the zodiac.

OLIVER. You're an artist like your bread friend?

ERIC (*with great bravado*). Oh much better than her, I hope.

OLIVER (*smiling*). Is that because you're not as successful?

ERIC (*deflated*). In probability, yes.

A slight pause.

Her work is merely shallow. I write as well. I think eventually I'll be known for my writing.

OLIVER. I can't keep up with you.

A slight pause.

ERIC. I have a small income left to me by a great-uncle. Unfortunately, it's not enough. I'm doing the *Vogue* illustrations for the money.

A slight pause.

OLIVER. What do you write?

ERIC. I have a novel about to be published.

OLIVER *looks surprised.*

OLIVER. What's it about?

ERIC. It's about a holiday I spent with my father on the south coast, when I was fourteen. About the people I met. Like the crazy school teacher.

A slight pause.

He tied my hands together one day rather savagely. For peering at him through the glass window of the hut where he was living. He was there for the summer, giving holidays to boys from the East End. He kept me tied for half an hour whilst he packed up to go home.

OLIVER. What had you done?

ERIC. Nothing as far as I knew. I suspect, like many people, he was smouldering inside. His veneer had snapped for a moment. I had watched him all summer, canoeing with the boys on the river.

A slight pause.

I must have challenged his authority. Like all tyrants, his form of punishment showed him up for what he really was.

OLIVER. What was that?

ERIC. A pederast.

A slight pause.

OLIVER. How can you be sure?

ERIC. I can't. I don't believe in absolute fact. I believe in the imagination.

A slight pause.

I was excited by being tied up like that.

OLIVER. Did you tell your father?

ERIC. Good Lord, no. He was busy with his newspaper in the lounge of the hotel.

A slight pause.

My accident has left me with bouts of impotence. I scrape together what I can from my youth.

OLIVER. Have you brothers and sisters?

ERIC. No, I would have liked them.

OLIVER. I have a sister and a brother.

ERIC. How old are they?

OLIVER. My sister's two years younger than me and my brother's eighteen. He now has his own decision to make.

A slight pause.

ERIC. My parents had me very late in their lives. My father was sixty when I was born. He was the rector of a small parish in Suffolk. I expect much of my life is a rebellion against their very ordinariness.

A slight pause.

My mother died when I was twelve and I was sent to school. My father's treats were those holidays on the south coast. I loved them, being by myself. And I so hated school.

OLIVER. Why?

ERIC. I was tyrannised.

OLIVER. By whom?

ERIC. Oh louts. I have to say I was rather pretty, which did
help. And of course, rather precocious, which didn't. It was
at school that I learnt to love my own sex.

OLIVER *has finished eating. He is looking at* ERIC.

I had two affairs, both with boys older than myself. One sat
me on his lap and undid the buttons of my trousers. I was
toasting his muffins when the request came. The other liked
to put me in the bath, which I think he enjoyed more than
me. But I was very clean for a few months.

ERIC *finishes his bread and cheese.*

OLIVER. If I was like you I don't think I could admit it to
anyone.

ERIC. But you're not, are you?

OLIVER. No.

ERIC *smiles.*

ERIC. I'm feeling quite euphoric today. You should see me
when I'm fed up. Or ill in bed because of my silly accident.

*There is the metallic 'swishing' sound of a flying-bomb as it
approaches from the distance.*

They hear it.

OLIVER *finds his jacket and takes a telescope from the
pocket. He stands up and looks through it towards the
horizon.*

Doodle-bug bombs?

OLIVER. Yes.

ERIC *stands up. He looks, shielding his eyes against the sun.*

I can see seven, eight, nine, ten. Eleven. Twelve.

OLIVER *offers the telescope to* ERIC. ERIC *looks through
it.*

ERIC. A few weekends ago I spent an evening in London with a friend of mine – the journalist, James Agate. A bizarre night in a shelter near the British Museum. Bohemian London talking about the latest books – writers striking deals with publishers. (*Suddenly.*) Take cover, one's coming down.

They lie flat on their stomachs, their hands covering their heads.

A pause.

There is a loud explosion from the distance.

They pick themselves up. ERIC *looks through the telescope.*

It looks to have landed near Hadlow. It's hit the church.

There is the 'whistling' sound of a bomb falling.

They dive for cover covering their heads.

There is a loud explosion, this time much closer.

They pick themselves up more slowly.

OLIVER. That one was too close for comfort.

ERIC. You'd have thought they'd have got the range by now.

OLIVER *takes the telescope. He looks through it.*

Where was it?

OLIVER. A few fields away.

He gives the telescope to ERIC. ERIC *looks.*

A slight pause.

Anything happening?

ERIC. They're running across the field towards it. They're all right.

ERIC *continues to look.*

The other ten doodle-bugs slowly die to silence.

The Squire's galloping across on his horse.

ERIC *lowers the telescope. He gives it back to* OLIVER. *They sit down again.*

A pause.

OLIVER. Is the friend – the friend you said you live with – is he your boyfriend?

ERIC. Yes. But we have separate beds. We antique together. That's to say my great pleasure is searching antique shops. I love collecting very small objects. I have a doll's house which I adore. At the moment I'm making the curtains from taffeta.

OLIVER. How many homosexuals d'you know?

ERIC. I say, I hope you don't think me sordid?

OLIVER. No.

ERIC. Gerard and I love each other. It's a very simple love. Which isn't to say that love is easy. We are very different characters. (*His hand above the cherries.*) Please.

OLIVER *takes a cherry. They begin to eat them.*

We do make love together. At times that is physically difficult for me.

OLIVER. What has your accident done?

ERIC. It's causing tuberculosis in my liver and intestines. I'm seeing another specialist next week, so all may be well.

A slight pause.

OLIVER. I'm so sorry.

A slight pause.

ERIC. What does your sister do?

OLIVER. She's just started teaching. My brother is just about to leave school.

ERIC. Are they nice?

OLIVER. Yes, we're a family that's very close.

ERIC. What's your father's work?

OLIVER. Funnily enough, he's a doctor. But a surgeon.

ERIC. What in?

OLIVER. Orthopaedics.

A slight pause.

He's a quiet man. You'd never think he was as recognised as he is.

A slight pause.

And very religious, too. Very open and honest, like I imagine Jesus would have been.

ERIC. D'you have the same convictions?

OLIVER. I'm a Quaker, yes.

ERIC. They're pacifists, aren't they? D'you go to the Meetings?

OLIVER. I try to. Not always. The nearest Meeting House is in Tunbridge Wells. It's difficult on the bus. We all went to Quaker schools.

ERIC. Which ones?

OLIVER. I to York. Richard to York. And Margaret to Great Ayton.

ERIC. Where's Great Ayton?

OLIVER. It's in Yorkshire, but further north.

A slight pause.

ERIC. I love looking at and sketching the details from churches.

OLIVER. Is that because your father was a rector?

ERIC. Perhaps it is, yes.

A slight pause.

I would very much like to go to a Meeting. Haven't you a bicycle?

OLIVER. No.

ERIC. You must get one.

OLIVER. I know.

ERIC. We could bicycle there together if you like?

OLIVER. Yes, certainly.

ERIC. There's a little shop in Tonbridge, there's no excuse.
You can ride?

OLIVER. Oh yes.

ERIC. I think it's rather odd, people who can't. They don't
really try.

A slight pause.

OLIVER. Your boyfriend – is he your first boyfriend?

ERIC (*after thinking for a moment*). Really, yes, he is.

OLIVER. How did you meet?

ERIC. He came to visit with another friend – not a boyfriend
friend. I asked him if he'd like to visit me again. Which he
did a few weeks later.

OLIVER. How did you get talking about it?

ERIC. About what?

OLIVER. How did you tell each other you were homosexual?

ERIC. I don't think we did, if I remember correctly. I think I
said one day about a soldier we'd been talking with – I said
I found him rather beautiful, which he was.

OLIVER. What did your boyfriend say?

ERIC. You have to understand he's coarser than me – he just
said he'd have liked to have taken his uniform off. And I
think the word was – fucked him.

A slight pause.

OLIVER. Thank you.

ERIC. It is easy for me to talk to you, we don't know each
other. I have many friends who know very little about me
because I've known them too long.

A slight pause.

Why did you choose to go on the land?

OLIVER. I didn't. In fact I started out in a hospital as a nurse's helper. At my tribunal that's what I asked for. It was very repetitive work. Maybe I haven't the right to say that?

A slight pause.

I don't want to make judgements on what I saw. I saw a lot of very ill men. Terrible injuries really, particularly the burns. They smell awful – the patient can smell himself.

There are only a few cherries left in the bottom of the bag. They have stopped eating them.

Then one day we had a German. I was asked to sit by him. They were very keen he didn't die. He had round-the-clock attention. No one else ever did.

A slight pause.

I think he'd been tortured. It looked to me very much like he had, he was in a terrible state. There was something unnatural about his injuries – can I say? It looked to me as if someone had pushed a needle into his eye. The cuts were very clean.

A slight pause.

I won't mention much else. It just looked to me as if a torturer had gone far too far. His fingers were missing. But I may be wrong.

A slight pause.

I wanted him to die. Which he did, thank the Lord. The anger unleashed on me. I went and told them I didn't want to work there any more.

A slight pause.

ERIC. Could it be what you imagined?

OLIVER. I didn't believe it could, before then.

ERIC. I don't believe it's so.

A slight pause.

ERIC *picks up the bag of cherries, he offers them to* OLIVER. OLIVER *takes a cherry in his fingers, he doesn't eat it.* ERIC *puts the bag down.*

They're yours, you have them.

ERIC *stands up.*

I'll have to go for a minute.

ERIC *exits.*

A pause.

ERIC *returns.*

OLIVER. Are you all right?

ERIC. No, I've been crying.

ERIC *sits down, as before.*

A pause.

OLIVER. I'm envious of you and your boyfriend. I think I wait too long until sex somehow becomes impossible. I would like to have sex with a boy.

ERIC *smiles.*

A slight pause.

OLIVER *eats the cherry he still has in his fingers. He picks up the bag, he offers the cherries to* ERIC. ERIC *eats one.*

They continue to eat the remaining cherries.

Which was the school you hated?

ERIC. Repton.

OLIVER. How did you begin to paint and write?

ERIC. I begged and pleaded with my father to be sent to art school.

OLIVER. Which you did?

ERIC. Yes, Goldsmiths in London.

OLIVER. Were you very young?

ERIC. I was seventeen.

OLIVER. Gosh, that was young. I can't draw.

ERIC. You could. It's just looking. Looking at something until you see nothing but what you're looking at. With that degree of concentration.

A slight pause.

OLIVER. Is that how you'd like to live? With that degree of purpose?

ERIC. Yes. But I get side-tracked.

ERIC *smiles.*

OLIVER. I know what you mean by looking closely at one thing. I suspect that's how we learn. Not by having a broad education in the traditional sense.

A slight pause.

I know being a conscientious objector has made me think the most I've ever thought about anything.

ERIC. How d'you feel now?

OLIVER (*after thinking for a moment*). Well, I haven't quite changed my mind.

ERIC. But nearly?

OLIVER. Very nearly. Let me ask you – would you be fighting?

ERIC *thinks.*

ERIC. I don't know. Yes. I don't believe in evil, you see.

OLIVER. I didn't used to.

A slight pause.

We're taught that God is good, that God will protect us. I used to believe that.

ERIC. Now you don't?

OLIVER. It's shaky. I've seen the consequences of evil.

ERIC. In the German?

OLIVER. Yes.

A slight pause.

ERIC. I was very pleased I never had to think about fighting.

OLIVER. My uncle was a conscientious objector in the last war, and actually spent it in prison. By a quirk of fate he's now working for the Government. He's an expert on Polish affairs and speaks Polish. There are rumours of terrible atrocities in Poland.

A slight pause.

If what he says is true, innocent people are being herded into labour camps. It's said, many may have been murdered for really no reason.

A slight pause.

Murder is surely wrong.

OLIVER *takes his jacket and searches through the pockets. He finds a photograph. He gives it to* ERIC.

I took that from his pocket.

ERIC. The German?

OLIVER. I presume it's his wife and family.

ERIC. And the dog.

A slight pause.

ERIC *gives the photograph back to* OLIVER. OLIVER *puts it back in his jacket pocket. In another pocket he finds a packet of cigarettes and some matches. He offers a cigarette to* ERIC.

Thank you.

OLIVER *lights both their cigarettes with a match.*

OLIVER. I don't normally smoke this brand. I have trouble getting my own.

ERIC. I didn't smoke at all until the woman in the post office made me.

OLIVER. How was that?

ERIC. I bought a packet for a friend one day. The next time I went in she'd bought some more in especially. I hadn't the heart to disappoint her.

OLIVER *smiles.*

I have to go in there because it's the only place to buy stamps. I suspect she does it to everyone.

OLIVER. I was at university in Nottingham. Near my lodgings there was a post office with the most amazing things. To find a new savings book she'd have to dig around amongst the potatoes. She couldn't add up either. I don't know how she made ends meet – many people I knew weren't honest about what she'd given them.

ERIC. It's a little like that in Tonbridge. I have a battle with her because she wants to be my friend.

ERIC *lies flat, leaning on his elbow.*

I think her son doesn't come home any more, something like that. I haven't a telephone in the cottage, hers is the nearest, people ring and leave messages.

OLIVER. Why don't you have one installed?

ERIC. Well I am, I hope.

OLIVER *lies on his side, on his elbow.*

OLIVER. How long have you been in Tonbridge?

ERIC. This is my third year. I've found a life now which is nice.

OLIVER. New places, new friendships, are difficult sometimes, aren't they? Where were you before?

ERIC. In hospital. I didn't finish Goldsmiths. The doctors advised me not to. I was born in Africa, though I don't remember because we left whilst I was tiny. I think I was rather a shock for my parents, after being childless so long. What did you read at Nottingham?

OLIVER. Chemistry. I've my final year still to do, it was interrupted, so I haven't my degree yet.

ERIC. I never even got the hang of the Bunsen burner. It was my copper sulphate which would never evaporate.

OLIVER (*smiling*). It has to interest you. I always liked the science side at school. I was good at it, too.

ERIC sits up. He opens his satchel and takes out the book proof of his novel.

ERIC. I came out to do this. (*Half showing him.*) It's the second proof of my novel. I have it to correct.

ERIC takes a pencil from the satchel.

In fact, there's some of my drawings in it, illustrating the chapter headings.

He gives the proof to OLIVER. OLIVER looks through it.

OLIVER. How long do they take you to do?

ERIC. I can do a drawing like one of those in an hour.

OLIVER continues to look.

They're trivial, decorative.

OLIVER. When can I buy a copy?

ERIC. It should be out in the autumn, for Christmas.

OLIVER gives the proof to ERIC.

OLIVER. I notice it has an introduction by Edith Sitwell.

ERIC. That's my publisher's doing. We hope she may help sell a few copies.

OLIVER. D'you know her?

ERIC. Yes, we had tea together in London. She was very sweet.

ERIC opens the proof in the middle, he has the pencil in his hand.

OLIVER. Did she like the book?

ERIC. She was kind enough to say so.

ERIC begins to correct the proof.

OLIVER. It makes my life with the cows look very paltry.

ERIC. Don't be silly.

ERIC *lies on his stomach, the book on the grass.*

When the war is eventually over will you go back and finish your degree?

OLIVER. Yes. Though I like the farm. I suspect there is a much bigger place for science in farming. It could be much more effective.

ERIC *leans on his elbow, he looks at* OLIVER.

They monitor nothing, so there's no record of performance. There's one cow in particular whose milk yield can't make her profitable.

A slight pause.

They're too old to hear of it really. Mr Whittle does know – but it's not the way he sees it.

ERIC. Have you argued with him?

OLIVER. Gently. I felt presumptuous doing that. So many things seem obvious to me because I know nothing about it. He's obsessive. I suppose many of us are obsessive, one way or another.

A slight pause.

Our obsessions are different.

A slight pause.

The German, he's my obsession at the moment. That's why I stole his photograph. I can see him without closing my eyes. I can even see his family.

A slight pause.

ERIC. I think you should go and enlist.

OLIVER. I think so, too.

A slight pause.

ERIC *returns to correcting his proof.*

ERIC. Just don't go and get killed.

OLIVER *laughs.*

The war's too real for me. I have my best experiences in my head. I believe in the reality of unconsummated experience.

A slight pause.

OLIVER. What's your friend doing in London?

ERIC *puts the pencil in the proof to mark the place. He sits up.*

ERIC. I've an exhibition he's busy with, at the Whitechapel. He's the only person I fully trust. He knows what I want.

OLIVER *nods.*

I shall go up on the train later in the week.

A slight pause.

I really ought to do this.

ERIC *opens the proof and continues to correct it.*

A slight pause.

OLIVER *lies back, he looks at the clear blue sky.*

A slight pause.

OLIVER. Have you seen the gypsies?

ERIC. Yes, I saw them from my bicycle. I love it at hop-picking time.

OLIVER. What happens then?

ERIC. Oh it's wonderful, I go and swop stories with them. Talk to the men on the stilts.

A slight pause.

ERIC *puts down the proof. He takes his braces off his shoulder and takes his shirt and vest off.*

The Londoners who know nothing about trees, sitting by their fires.

OLIVER *leans on his elbow, looking at* ERIC.

ERIC *takes his shoes and socks off. He unfastens his trousers, and pushes them off with his underpants.*

I'm teaching a group of evacuees about the countryside. We share cigarettes together.

ERIC *picks up the proof and continues to correct it.*

OLIVER *lies back.*

OLIVER. I thought we were going swimming?

ERIC. I'd like to in a minute, wouldn't you?

A slight pause.

OLIVER *sits up. He unfastens his trousers and pushes them off with his underpants. He lies back, looking at the hot sun.*

ERIC *is correcting the proof.*

The End.

Two
LOST

Characters

MAY APPLETON
GEOFFREY CHURCH

A terraced house in Redcar, Cleveland. June 1982.

The front room of a small terraced house in Redcar, Cleveland. June 1982.

A doorway; a rug on the floor; a grandfather clock which ticks loudly; two newly upholstered armchairs; a small table on which is a vase of freshly cut flowers, and a small transistor radio. On the floor is a newspaper opened at the crossword, a dictionary and a biro. There is an empty coffee-mug.

MAY APPLETON *is sitting knitting. She is listening to a radio play.*

MAY *is a small, plumpish woman of sixty-one. She has a round face and her hair is newly set. She is wearing her best summer dress with her best shoes.* GEOFFREY CHURCH *is standing behind her in the open doorway.*

GEOFFREY *is a tall, slender man of thirty-one. He is wearing his lieutenant's naval uniform.*

GEOFFREY. Mrs Appleton.

  MAY *jumps with a start. She turns.*

  I'm so sorry, the door was open.

MAY (*standing up with her knitting*). I'm busy givin' the house a blow through before our Gillian comes round. Jim an' 'is tobacco seem t'get everywhere these days.

GEOFFREY. I'm Geoffrey Church. I'm a friend of Ian's.

MAY. A friend of our Ian's?

GEOFFREY. Yes. May I come in?

MAY. Gillian is comin' with the kiddies at any moment.

GEOFFREY. May I, please?

MAY. Yer'd better come in then.

  GEOFFREY *enters the room.* MAY *puts her knitting on the chair and turns the radio off.*

If yer've come t'see Jim he's down at the Legion playin' 'is snooker. Gillian's comin' with the kiddies f'tea. It's the little one's birthday.

GEOFFREY. Have you not heard from Portsmouth, Mrs Appleton?

MAY: We haven't heard anythin'.

GEOFFREY. Someone should have been in touch with you.

MAY. It's our Ian?

GEOFFREY. I'm so sorry no one's told you.

MAY. Yer'd better sit yerself down.

   GEOFFREY *sits in the other chair.*

GEOFFREY. Why don't you sit down, Mrs Appleton.

   MAY *sits.*

   Silence, except for the ticking of the clock.

MAY. D'yer want to wait for Jim? D'yer want a cup of tea?

   A slight pause.

   We haven't heard from Ian for over five years, yer know.

GEOFFREY. He was on *Glamorgan,* Mrs Appleton.

MAY. Has he been killed?

GEOFFREY. Yes.

   A slight pause.

MAY. The last time we heard anythin' from 'im he was on that aircraft-carrier the *Hermes.*

GEOFFREY. He transferred to *Glamorgan* eighteen months ago.

MAY. We thought he must be there, or thereabouts.

GEOFFREY. I'm so very sorry.

   A slight pause.

MAY. It's the television given Jim the snooker. It has a lot of men, hasn't it?

GEOFFREY. Yes.

MAY. Those with time on their hands. We don't rent.

A slight pause.

I've been livin' with the television on, an' the radio. We thought with 'im bein' on the *Hermes,* we thought well, it's an important boat, they won't want that to be hit. The littler ones don't matter so much, do they?

GEOFFREY. No.

MAY. Ian wanted to get on in the Navy, he had to move about. Go to the ships 'e was told.

GEOFFREY. Yes.

MAY. Before the *Hermes* he was on the *Bronington.* That was with the Prince of Wales, yer know, with Prince Charles?

GEOFFREY. Yes.

MAY. Ian was a midshipman, or some such thing. He talked all about Prince Charles. We laughed about it.

A slight pause.

I felt proud in my own way. Just a little thing like that. It led you to imagine things, didn't it?

GEOFFREY. I was on *Bronington*, too.

MAY (*pleased*). Were you?

GEOFFREY. Yes, with Ian.

MAY. Were your mum an' dad pleased for you?

GEOFFREY. Very much so.

MAY (*confidentially*). It's not a secret – I had never felt so proud before. I know Ian thought we were bein' silly makin' the fuss we did. But yer children matter to you, don't they?

GEOFFREY. Yes.

MAY. Ian wasn't good in that way – lettin' other people get enjoyment from what he was doin'. Yer'd've thought 'is parents, wouldn't you?

GEOFFREY. Yes.

MAY. He must've thought it was a lot to ask. I don't know why.

A slight pause.

No, I don't know why. Something in his make-up.

A slight pause.

Have you come a long way to come an' see us?

GEOFFREY. My family live in the Peak District, Mrs Appleton. I travelled there yesterday, and came away after an early lunch.

MAY. Are you hungry?

GEOFFREY. No.

MAY. I have some sandwiches cut. Or a pastry. You'd be most welcome.

GEOFFREY. No, really, thank you.

A slight pause.

MAY. It's Alexander's birthday. He's three. Katharine is seven. They're shooting up.

A slight pause.

Are you from a Navy family?

GEOFFREY. Yes, I am, very much so.

MAY. I know that's true a lot of the time in the Navy, with all its customs.

GEOFFREY. My father was Vice-Admiral.

MAY. That's very high up, isn't it?

GEOFFREY (*nervously*). Yes.

GEOFFREY *plays with his fingers.*

It's a hard act to follow. I feel it very often.

MAY. It is a pressure for you, isn't it? I can imagine.

GEOFFREY. Yes.

GEOFFREY *plays with his fingers.*

My grandfather was Admiral of the Fleet.

MAY. Was that during the war?

GEOFFREY. Yes.

MAY. Jim was in the Air Force. On the ground. That's where we met up.

A slight pause.

I always think it must be rotten on family life, being high up in anything. That's what I imagine.

GEOFFREY. It is indeed so. I have a family now, with two little girls. One must make very positive decisions. The Navy is not terribly understanding of family life.

A slight pause.

You are right, Mrs Appleton. Just last evening I was arguing with my father. He does not comprehend my mother's feelings, let alone my wife's.

A slight pause.

Though my mother is silent on the issue.

A slight pause.

I've just been appointed to Chatham on the Flag Officer's staff. It's a shore job in the supply department. He says all I'm doing is dishing out Mars Bars – which up to a point is true.

A slight pause.

My father's a stranger to me. I love my children.

A slight pause.

I don't know how much Ian talked to you about the Navy?

MAY. Did 'e talk t'you?

GEOFFREY. Considerably at times, yes. We were very close. He loved the life in a way I never shall.

MAY. You know more than me.

They are looking at one another.

Yer can't upset us any more about Ian. He wasn't the son
we wanted.

GEOFFREY. I think you're being very hard on him.

MAY: Not as hard as he was on us. He's destroyed his father.

A slight pause.

Some things women cope with better than men. I'd say 'e'd
only hurt me very deeply.

A slight pause.

Because he's so hurt his father over the last few years. And
he's really hurt me as well.

A slight pause.

It's not fair what Ian's gone an' done.

MAY *hides a tear.*

He's been good-riddance-to-bad-rubbish for so long.

Silence, except for the ticking of the clock.

MAY *looks up, she has a single tear in her eye.*

He was my son.

GEOFFREY *looks down.*

He didn't even write, you know. It wouldn't have cost him
much. A piece of paper. A stamp. You were his friend. Why
did he do that?

GEOFFREY *looks up.*

GEOFFREY. I don't know, Mrs Appleton.

MAY. You can't have been his friend then.

A slight pause.

GEOFFREY. We talked about our families.

MAY. You've come all this way. Don't you owe it to me?

A slight pause.

I think you do owe it.

A slight pause.

Maybe we weren't the parents he wanted. I don't know.
I know we tried.

A slight pause.

We mustn't've been the parents he wanted. Why didn't 'e
try and tell us. 'E was a sensitive boy, we would've listened.

A slight pause.

I can't believe we could be so wrong in his eyes.

A slight pause.

Now you're the only person who can tell me.

A slight pause.

GEOFFREY. Ian was selfish, Mrs Appleton. He used to talk
about what it was like coming home. He found it
claustrophobic. I was always rather envious of the way it
sounded.

A slight pause.

He changed from the person I knew at university. I argued
with him a good deal about his ambition.

A slight pause.

When we were midshipmen together it was easy. I don't
think he thought about his career until it became evident
that he was going to do very well. He was well liked. He
was good, Mrs Appleton. He wasn't in a room long before
he was the one taking the attention.

A slight pause.

He didn't even need to compete, he just had what it takes.
As early as Dartmouth he was the star.

MAY. Ian was a bright boy. It's no secret – 'e used t'surprise
me how clever he was. Mebbe that says a lot about us as a
family.

A slight pause.

He was such a quiet boy. Never in any trouble. Yer'd go to 'is school an' the teachers'd greet yer like friends. 'Is dad used t'say it was uncanny. When it came to it they wanted 'im to stop another year and do those Oxford exams. Ian said, no, he wouldn't. It was the first time I saw him bother a teacher. Quiet people often have a stubborn streak, don't they?

GEOFFREY. Yes.

MAY. He didn't ask us about the Navy, yer know. He told us he thought it would be right for him. It's that what's upset Jim – his never asking advice. He could have done, couldn't he? He could have pretended?

GEOFFREY. Yes.

MAY. Jim took against 'im a bit after that. It'd been brewing, yer know.

A slight pause.

I think if the truth's told, Jim's been jealous of our Ian. From Ian bein' a teenager, I can see the signs. Jim never had the chances. It was different then – the war and everything. Boys like Jim had to go and fight. What choices had they?

A slight pause.

As Ian rose up in the Navy it just made it worse. Jim saw him succeedin', yer know. Ian couldn't share it with 'is dad. I don't know why. That's all 'is dad ever wanted.

A slight pause.

I did tell Jim 'e couldn't live 'is life through Ian. I knew it wasn't fair, the way things were going. Jim wouldn't have it. Jim always knew best. It didn't matter what about. Ian's silence just grated with 'im.

A slight pause.

Jim wanted agreement, you see. Jim's never thought very highly of himself. That's one of the things I love about him. He's not like a lot of men.

A slight pause.

Did you know Ian hadn't been home for five years?

GEOFFREY. Yes.

MAY. What must you think about us?

Silence, except for the ticking of the clock.

I think if Ian had realised how all his father wanted was reassurance, it would have been all right. That's part of becoming an adult, isn't it? Realising things like that. In lots of ways Ian was still a kiddy.

A slight pause.

I suppose when you're away at sea you only have yourself to think about. It has a discipline, doesn't it, that takes care of everything. Makes sure you have what you need. Ian used to say to me it was surprisin' how easy it all was.

A slight pause.

Yes, I think he was a child in lots of ways.

A slight pause.

Jim won't talk about Ian. This is goin' t'knock him for six. It's not fair on little Alexander on his birthday. Me in my best clothes.

GEOFFREY. It's an important war, Mrs Appleton.

MAY. I don't think we know, do we? All we know is that people are being killed.

A slight pause.

GEOFFREY. I simply meant that Naval men like Ian are doing their duty, in very difficult circumstances.

MAY. Who will remember the Falklands War?

A slight pause.

GEOFFREY. I'm sorry you feel like that, Mrs Appleton.

MAY. His duty was to us, to 'is parents. He didn't even let us know where he was. He could have been anywhere for all we knew. We were left to wonder. Don't tell me it's his duty to go getting himself killed doing some stupid silly thing. I've had time to think about it these last few weeks. Let me tell you, I've thought about nothing else. I've thought where was Ian, every single day.

Silence, except for the ticking of the clock.

It isn't fair, not fair at all.

A slight pause.

I only know one thing – surely, if he thought there was a chance of 'im being killed he would have come an' seen us. Or posted a letter. Even Ian.

A slight pause.

This is torture for me, I wish you'd leave, please.

GEOFFREY *stands up. He looks at* MAY. *He walks to the doorway, he stops and turns.*

Silence, except for the ticking of the clock.

MAY *looks up at him.*

GEOFFREY. I can't leave like this, Mrs Appleton.

MAY. No.

GEOFFREY. There are so many things I wanted to say. Ian was married. I don't think you knew. I really came here on behalf of his wife. No one wants it left like this.

A slight pause.

It may be that I shouldn't have come. I did expect you to know about his death. That isn't my fault.

MAY *stands up.*

I feel terrible at the moment. Terrible for you. Terrible for myself. And Hilary his wife –

A slight pause.

You will have to forgive us, we thought we were doing our best.

A slight pause.

I really didn't want to upset you.

A slight pause.

MAY. Yes, I can see that now. I'm sometimes very slow. Ian must've found us slow, did 'e?

GEOFFREY. I don't know, Mrs Appleton. Ian became very snobbish.

MAY. Snobbish?

GEOFFREY. I think so, yes.

A slight pause.

MAY. If he'd jus' posted us a letter, yer know.

A slight pause.

I feel like I hate him, an' yet I still love 'im at the same time. Isn't it awful t'have t'say yer might hate yer own son?

A slight pause.

I feel that about Jim sometimes.

A slight pause.

I suppose 'avin' what might be hateful feelings is a part of having love, isn't it? It shows that deep in yer heart yer still care about the person concerned.

A slight pause.

GEOFFREY. Yes.

MAY. Which part of the ship was Ian in?

GEOFFREY. I gather he was on the flight deck.

MAY. He wasn't in the water then?

GEOFFREY. No.

MAY. It must be awful t'drown, mustn't it?

GEOFFREY. Yes.

MAY. It must be like suffocating. Would it 'appen quickly, 'im bein' on the flight deck.

GEOFFREY. Yes.

MAY. He wouldn't know too much about it then.

GEOFFREY. No.

MAY. This wife he's got?

GEOFFREY. Hilary.

MAY. Yes. Did this Hilary ask you to come an' see us?

GEOFFREY. Yes.

MAY. She must be really upset, poor soul.

GEOFFREY. She is, terribly upset.

MAY. D'you know her well?

GEOFFREY. I know her very well, Mrs Appleton.

MAY. Will you say something to her from us?

GEOFFREY. Yes, I will.

MAY. I feel very sorry for her.

A slight pause.

GEOFFREY. Hilary is my sister, Mrs Appleton.

MAY. Your sister?

GEOFFREY. Yes.

MAY. Our Ian was married to your sister? What must you think of us?

GEOFFREY *goes to* MAY.

GEOFFREY. Please.

MAY. What must you be thinking after everything I've said?

GEOFFREY. Please.

MAY. You should've told me, shouldn't you? Instead of lettin' me go on.

GEOFFREY. I should. I somehow couldn't.

MAY. You should've said when you came through the door. It should've been the first thing.

GEOFFREY. I agree, I'm so sorry. Please.

MAY. What must you think?

> MAY *sits.*

> GEOFFREY *sits.*

GEOFFREY. I couldn't find the right moment.

> *A slight pause.*

MAY. We didn't even know our Ian was married, yer know.

GEOFFREY. No.

MAY. He had a girlfriend at school, but it came to nothin' when 'e went away. We hoped he would get married one day. It's not a life bein' on your own, is it?

GEOFFREY. No.

MAY. When you're young and your life's before you, you need someone to share it with.

GEOFFREY. Yes.

> *A slight pause.*

MAY. How long had they been married?

GEOFFREY. They were married four years ago.

MAY. Four years. Had they a home together?

GEOFFREY. Yes, in Chichester.

MAY. A nice house and everything?

GEOFFREY. A very nice house in a quiet cul-de-sac.

MAY. An' they were happy together?

GEOFFREY. Very happy indeed.

MAY. You should have told me. It was wrong not to.

> *A slight pause.*

> But you didn't tell me, so that's that.

GEOFFREY. Yes.

MAY. It's forgotten, isn't it? We'll know what we said but we won't tell Jim.

GEOFFREY. Yes.

A slight pause.

What about, Mrs Appleton?

MAY. If we could tell 'im all about your sister and the marriage – tell 'im all the good things, not the bad things. Jim will like that. It's wrong to dwell on the bad things, isn't it?

GEOFFREY. Yes.

MAY. If we say Ian wanted to write to us, but was too busy. If we say Ian's responsibilities were so big that he just didn't have time, Jim will understand that.

GEOFFREY. Yes.

MAY. I know it's a little lie, but sometimes that's better isn't it?

GEOFFREY. Yes.

MAY. If we say he died fighting for his country, which he did, we can be proud of that, can't we?

GEOFFREY. Yes.

MAY. As his mum an' dad we can be very, very proud of that.

GEOFFREY. Yes, Mrs Appleton.

MAY. It is important, this war. I am proud of Ian.

MAY *and* GEOFFREY *are looking at one another.*

The End.

Interval.

Three

MAKING NOISE QUIETLY

Characters

HELENE ENSSLIN
ALAN TADD
SAM

A wood in the Black Forest, Germany, August 1986.

Scene One: late afternoon.
Scene Two: evening.

Scene One

A wood in the Black Forest of south-west Germany. August 1986.

The late afternoon sunlight is shining through the dense growths of pine trees. There is a thick, pineneedled forest floor.

HELENE ENSSLIN *is sitting on a stool painting in poster-colours at an easel.*

HELENE *is a tall, thin, dignified woman of fifty-seven who has her long hair in a bun. She is wearing a good loose-fitting summer dress.*

SAM *is standing at her shoulder watching her paint.*

SAM *is a small, thin, scrappy boy of eight. He is wearing trousers, a shirt and a grey jumper. The sleeves of his shirt and jumper are rolled up to his elbows. His arms are mucky and there is writing on them.*

ALAN TADD *is lying on the ground a short distance away.*

ALAN is *a small, squat, muscular man of thirty-one with an angular face and short hair. He is wearing jeans, a teeshirt and a jumper.*

HELENE. Pick up the water jar for me.

> SAM *bends down and carefully picks it up in both hands.* HELENE *washes her brush.*

You see how I like to keep looking at what I am painting?

SAM *nods.*

This landscape has a feeling for me I wish to capture. But it vary with my moods, you understand? So always the feeling is different, so always the painting is different.

> SAM *carefully puts the water jar on the ground, he picks up a small rag. He takes* HELENE's *brush from her and dries it.*

When I was a very small girl this forest was a playground for us children. Then it was castles and little girls who slept for a hundred years. For my brothers it was white knights fighting demons.

SAM *gives her the brush. He squats down at the box of poster-paints. He looks up at her.*

Find me the blue.

SAM *finds a blue.*

Not the light blue, the dark blue.

SAM *finds the dark blue. He stands up, he gives it to her, he keeps the light blue in his hand.*

HELENE *paints. When she isn't looking,* SAM *puts the pot of light blue into his trouser pocket. He squats down.*

A slight pause.

SAM *takes out the felt-tip pen which is clipped into one of his socks and he writes on his arm with it.*

Where is your notepad got to?

SAM *shrugs, he continues to write.* ALAN *looks up.*

ALAN. 'Aven' I told yer not t'do that?

SAM (*an almost inaudible moan*).

HELENE. All his notepads have feet.

ALAN. Eh!

SAM (*a loud sharp angry moan*).

ALAN. You'll be the one screamin' when we 'ave t'wash it off.

ALAN *lies back.* SAM *finishes writing, he shows* HELENE *what he has written.*

HELENE. Of course, but not today.

ALAN. What's 'e say?

HELENE. He is asking me if I will paint him.

ALAN (*leaning on his elbow*). Yer a vain little basket, aren't yer, Sam? That's my fault, like, I was meant to ask yer. 'E's been goyn on about nothin' else.

SAM *clips the felt-tip pen back into his sock.* ALAN *sits up.*

Did yer ever carve yer initials in 'em?

HELENE. What is that?

ALAN. The trees, yer know. A reckoned we could go an' look for it.

HELENE. No, I did not. It is in the city parks where this bad thing happen.

ALAN. I used to like.

HELENE. In the country we respect nature.

ALAN. Yer jus' think it does 'em 'arm, it doesn't.

HELENE. I am not sure.

ALAN. Yer wrong.

HELENE. It leaves signs of people where there should not be.

ALAN. Yeh, all right. Yer wrong though.

HELENE. I think you must lose the argument.

ALAN. Who said?

HELENE. I think it is the way when you do a wrong thing.

ALAN. Yer must be jokin', aren't yer?

HELENE (*a hidden smile*). I do not joke, I speak seriously.

A slight pause.

ALAN. A d'know what yer talkin' about.

HELENE. I say when you do a wrong thing, you lose the argument.

ALAN. 'Ave it your way, you win.

A slight pause.

HELENE. I only win when you understand what I say about morality.

ALAN. Yeh, I'm not very moral, though.

HELENE. There you are wrong again, Alan.

ALAN *lies back.*

A short silence.

ALAN. I couldn't give a fuck t'tell yer the truth.

A slight pause.

HELENE. A fuck?

ALAN. Yeh, a fuck, it's rude t'you.

A slight pause.

HELENE. We have words in Germany, too.

ALAN. Yeh, well, fuck is English. It means fuck off.

A slight pause.

HELENE. If you are not happy, why do you not leave? I am not your gaoler here.

SAM (*a long moan*).

SAM *starts to panic. He has a tantrum very quickly, he stands up and stamps his foot.*

A long loud screech.

HELENE *touches* SAM *on the shoulder.*

HELENE. It is all right, Sam.

SAM *looks imploringly towards* ALAN.

SAM (*a lot of short, sharp moans which beg the answer to a question*).

ALAN (*sitting up*). Yeh, we're stayin', kid.

SAM *stops. He squats down. He picks up a paint-brush and cleans it with the rag. One of his legs shakes a little.*

A slight pause. HELENE *begins to paint again.*

A slight pause. ALAN *lies back.*

I d'know why the kid likes yer so much. Beats me.

A slight pause.

Mind you, 'e likes owt. As long as 'e gets 'is own way. Isn't it, Sam?

SAM *is watching* HELENE *paint. His leg continues to twitch.*

If I got me own way as much as 'im I'd be laughin'. Fuck me, I'd do owt a wanted.

A slight pause.

I'd be fuckin' the world if a got me way as much as 'im. Eh, Sam?

SAM (*an almost inaudible moan*).

ALAN. Beats me why you wan' us 'ere.

HELENE. Now I need the light blue.

HELENE *screws the top on the dark blue; she gives it to* SAM. SAM *puts it in the box. He searches for the light blue. He looks up and shrugs.*

It was there a moment ago.

SAM *looks again. He shrugs.*

Where can it have got to, Sam?

SAM *shrugs.*

ALAN *looks up. He jumps up.*

ALAN. 'Ave you taken it yer little bleeder?

SAM (*a loud, sharp screech*).

ALAN *goes to* SAM *and grabs him.* SAM *stamps his foot and struggles to get away.*

A series of ear-piercing screeches from SAM.

ALAN *turns* SAM *upside down. He shakes him by the legs. The pot of paint, an antique gold ring, a teaspoon, a tube of lipstick, miscellaneous buttons, a silver brooch, a badge and a piece of string are amongst the things which tumble out of his trouser pockets.*

SAM *struggles.*

ALAN *continues to shake until nothing more falls. He drops* SAM *down onto his back and whacks him hard across the backside.*

ALAN. Take 'er it back.

SAM *curls up into a ball, he is silent. He rocks violently.*

ALAN *picks up the pot of paint, he gives it to* HELENE. HELENE *takes it.*

HELENE. I must ask you, did you never put some articles into your pockets?

ALAN (*much quieter*). Yeh, well, 'e does it all the time. Everywhere we bleedin' go. Whatever 'e fancies 'e just takes.

He bends down, he touches SAM *on the head.*

Sorry, Sam.

He straightens up.

'Ow else is 'e gonna learn what's right an' what's wrong?

HELENE. I must ask you never to treat the boy that way again in front of me.

ALAN. Yeh, all right. I'm sorry.

He bends down, he touches SAM *on the head.*

Sorry, Sam.

SAM *moves quickly. He collects up all the other things and stuffs them back into his trouser pockets. He curls up again into a ball. He rocks.*

'E goes like a hedgehog when 'e gets annoyed. He can kick an' punch an' all. He's like a little tiger. Yer should see it when we 'ave t'wash 'is writin' off. A reckon 'e thinks 'is writing is part of 'im. Eh, Sam?

SAM (*a quiet moan of agreement*).

ALAN. 'E gets over it quick, yer know. Usually. Just the odd time like 'e goes off on 'is own an' yer left wonderin' where 'e's got to. When the little devil met you, yer know – then we'd 'ad a row, 'e'd gone off on one of 'is jaunts. 'Adn't yer, Sam?

SAM (*a quiet grunt of agreement*).

ALAN (*bending down to him*). When you met the lady. It's been good ever since, 'asn't it?

SAM (*a quiet grunt of agreement*).

    ALAN *straightens up.*

ALAN. He either tekks a shine t'yer, or 'e doesn't. You, 'e took a shine to, like. He's told me.

    SAM *is rocking, still tightly curled into the ball.*

    We both 'ave, yer know. We've told each other. We reckon yer've bin good to us. Me, I've a temper like a witch, that's all. The boy needs a mother really. Don't yer, Sam?

    SAM *is silent.*

    'E likes women. A reckon when 'e's older 'e's gonna be a right lady-lover. Aren't yer, kid?

SAM (*a quiet grunt of agreement*).

ALAN. See.

HELENE. I see.

ALAN. I'm not 'is dad, yer know. Not 'is real dad like. I mean I've been lumbered with the little sod. He's like from my wife's first marriage. We never 'ad kids – we never got the bloody chance, she was off inside three months. My bleedin' wife. Off with another bloody geezer. Another fuckin' soldier. She can go fuck herself for all I care. I mean, how fuckin' dare she. Fuckin' soldiers, they're all pox. Ran off with my bleedin' sergeant and left me wi' the kid. Fuckin' marriage, I never 'ad one.

    A slight pause.

HELENE. But you still love your wife?

ALAN. What's love? Don' ask me.

A slight pause.

Yeh, I've been hurt, like. If I see 'er again I'll fuckin' kill 'er.

HELENE. And Sam?

ALAN. Like a say, 'e's not my kid.

HELENE. But you use Sam to get back at your wife?

ALAN. You must be jokin'. She didn't wan' 'im. D'yer think I'd be standin' ere if there was anywhere for 'im to go? Poor sod.

HELENE. But his real father, where is he?

ALAN. The army tried to find 'im. When the' did, 'e didn't want t'know, like. Bastard.

HELENE. So it is you who have Sam?

ALAN. Yeh, for the moment.

HELENE. But for how long is this moment?

ALAN. The' gave us three months' leave, like, t'try an' sort it out. All I've done is mooch about.

HELENE. Why is this?

ALAN. A don't know what t' do. Jus' keepin' 'im washed and fed tekks all me time. A mean the kid's a handful. Yer can see that, can't yer?

HELENE. Yes.

ALAN. I mean a know it's not 'is fault. Is it, Sam?

SAM (*a grunt of agreement*).

ALAN. What do a do when no one wants 'im? You tell us, mekk us all feel easier?

HELENE. But you do not want Sam, no?

A slight pause.

ALAN. You ask a question, don't yer?

SAM *uncurls himself. He takes his felt-tip pen from his sock and writes on his arm. He shows his arm to* ALAN.

Yeh, a know son, a know.

HELENE. What has Sam written?

ALAN *shows* HELENE SAM*'s arm.*

ALAN. The little bleeder wants t'stay with me.

SAM *clips his pen back into his sock. He curls up again. He rocks.*

The boy's dead loyal, yer know. It amazes me, I don't understand it, considerin' what a do to him.

HELENE. Do you treat the boy in this way quite often?

ALAN. A don't mean to, like, it just 'appens yer know.

HELENE. You hit Sam?

ALAN. Yeh, a do. Like a say, it's just me temper. The little sod provokes me. I aren't fit to be 'is dad really.

ALAN *pulls up* SAM's *jumper and shirt.* SAM's *back is covered in red weals.* SAM *struggles.*

That was from two days ago before 'e ran off an' met you, like.

HELENE. What had he done?

ALAN. He was writin' rude things on 'is arm, telling me to fuck off.

SAM *tucks his shirt back into his trousers. He rocks in the ball again.*

I alwez tell mesel' I'll never do it again.

HELENE. But you do?

ALAN. Yeh. The kid comes back. A reckon 'e like us. Fuck knows why.

HELENE. But you always apologise to Sam?

ALAN. Oh, yeh, a do that. We're daggers drawn 'til we've made up.

HELENE. But it is you who has made up?

ALAN. Yeh. 'E's just a kid, yer know. Yer can't expect 'im to do that.

HELENE. Sam, he has never hurt you?

ALAN. 'E can lash out a bit, but it doesn't hurt like.

HELENE. That is not what I mean by hurt.

ALAN. What d'yer mean then?

HELENE. I am looking for the reason why you hit Sam so.

ALAN (*aggressively*). 'Cos I'm fuckin' mad.

HELENE. But that is too easy for you. It explain away everything for you. It keep your life the simple way so you have to do nothing.

ALAN. Fuck off!

HELENE. See, now we have the demonstration of nothing.

ALAN. Go an' fuck off.

ALAN *squats down. He pulls* SAM *towards him.* SAM *moans and sucks his thumb, he is still in the ball.*

HELENE. Now I see who is the child.

ALAN. Yer can't hurt me.

HELENE. But I am hurting you, no?

ALAN (*quietly*). Get lost.

HELENE. I will not, Alan.

ALAN. Fuck off.

A slight pause.

HELENE. When I see this boy on his own, wandering through the trees, I have pity for him. He looked so sad there, a little skeleton in his hurt. I think you should have pity, too.

A slight pause.

It is not the way to beat a child until he bleeds because we are the one who is hurt.

ALAN (*screaming*). Fuck off.

A short silence.

HELENE *stands up. She goes to* ALAN.

SAM (*a disconcerted moan*).

SAM *changes position, he gets more comfortable with his head on* ALAN*'s leg. He is still.*

A short silence.

HELENE *kneels on the ground.* ALAN *looks at her.*

ALAN. Yeh. What do a do though?

HELENE. I, too, find it difficult sometimes. But we must try with ourselves, no?

ALAN. I just hate, me, that's the trouble. I 'ave done, right since bein' a kid. Blind hate, yer know. I remember tryin' t'kick the hell out of a wall. All it did was hurt back, more. A couldn't even laugh about it. When I was about eight, 'is age like, I learnt yer could hit people. An' I enjoyed it. I got away with it. Yeh, I got away with it.

A slight pause.

Been gettin' away with it. Suddenly this little nipper comes along.

SAM (*a grunt*).

ALAN. Yeh, you. Half the time a feel like bein' nice to 'im, half the time a don't.

SAM *sits up. He squats. He takes his felt-tip pen and writes on his arm. He shows his arm to* ALAN.

He wants t'know 'ow long yer've been livin' 'ere like?

SAM *looks at* HELENE. *He puts his felt-tip back in his sock. He bobs up and down on his haunches.*

HELENE. This house, Sam, it has always been my family's house. We used to call it the shooting lodge. My father used to like to shoot the deer in the forests.

SAM *holds his hand out to* ALAN *like a gun. He makes a shooting noise. He falls back in a sitting position onto* ALAN. ALAN *holds him.*

Yes. But my real home, with my brothers and sisters, was in Berlin. This was the lodge where we came for our summers.

ALAN. It must've been great.

HELENE. It has changed very, very little. Of course I have painted the house, and built my studio in the old barn.

SAM *takes his felt-tip pen and quickly writes on his arm.* ALAN *watches.*

ALAN. 'E wants t'know if you're rich.

HELENE *smiles.*

HELENE. I do not know what to say. Yes, I am rich. My father he owned a big department store in Berlin. It was full of the fashions and furs. This lodge is the same for me now. I have a flat not in Berlin, but in Cologne which is where I run my business. This painting it is only my hobby, I am a business woman. This is my summer, for three months I like very much to paint.

SAM *points to himself.*

SAM (*a series of insistent short, sharp grunts*).

ALAN. She said she would, didn't she. Tomorrow.

SAM *puts his felt-tip in his sock.*

HELENE. Tomorrow I will paint Sam as long as he is good.

ALAN. Yer'll be good, won't yer, Sam?

SAM *lifts his leg, he lets it fall.*

That means yes. (*Looking at* SAM.) If yer don't wet the bed tonight, the lady will paint yer.

HELENE. That is not what I said. I think we should draw a
line on what is good. Good means not taking any more of
my private possessions.

SAM *lifts his leg, he lets it fall.*

ALAN. It's a deal.

HELENE. This agreement is important, Sam.

SAM *lifts his leg, he lets it fall.*

Good, then I shall trust you.

SAM *lifts his leg, he lets it fall.*

ALAN. 'E sez 'e trusts you.

HELENE *stands up and returns to her easel.* ALAN *runs
his fingers through* SAM's *hair.*

A reckon yer hair needs washin', son. It's like a grease
factory.

SAM *lifts his leg, he lets it fall.*

'Is leg alwez takes over when 'e's gettin' tired.

SAM *moves. He squats on his haunches, bobbing up and
down very slightly.* ALAN *squats on his haunches.* SAM
watches HELENE.

We thought yer must be an artist like, yer know a painter? It
seems dead good what yer do.

HELENE *smiles.*

HELENE. No, my business is in fabrics. I weave and print
cloth and wool. This began in a very small way for me,
doing the designs, selling my fabric to the shop. Then I
open the shop and it grow from there. Today I have a group
of designers who work for me. But I too, I too continue.
Today we are a big concern, with a shop each in all the big
towns. Soon we go to Europe. A shop in Paris, a shop in
London. For my nine months I work very hard, Alan.

HELENE *rubs her hand up and down her legs.*

ALAN. Yer cold?

HELENE. My leg is a little cold.

ALAN. D'yer wan' us t'get yer something from the house?

HELENE. No, it does not matter.

> ALAN *takes a packet of cigarettes and a lighter from his jeans pocket. He goes to her.*

ALAN. D'yer want one of these?

HELENE. No, no thank you.

ALAN. I don't know when yer smoke an' when yer don't.

HELENE. I like to have a cigarette after a meal.

> ALAN *lights a cigarette. He puts the packet and the lighter back in his pocket.*

ALAN. Sorry about 'is wettin' the bed, yer know.

> SAM *lifts his leg, he lets it fall.*

'E just alwez 'as.

HELENE. It is no problem to wash the sheets through.

ALAN. The doctor gave us one of those alarm things. It rings when he pees. What 'appened to it, Sam?

> SAM *is silent.*

Any road, 'e didn't like it.

> SAM *holds up his hand with two fingers outstretched.*

SAM (*a short moan, a request*).

> ALAN *puts the cigarette between* SAM's *fingers.* ALAN *sits down.* SAM *falls back onto him.* SAM *smokes.* SAM *is still, he is completely relaxed.*

ALAN. His mother couldn't stand 'im peein'. She used t'mekk 'im lick it up, didn't she, Sam?

> SAM *lifts his leg, he lets it fall.*

Thing is about kids, they don't forget, d'they? I mean yer get stuff comin' back at yer weeks later. 'E 'asn't forgot 'is mother.

SAM *lifts his leg, he lets it fall.*

Shiz a fuckin' cow really. I mean 'ow d'yer teach a kid right an' wrong by doin' stuff like that? At least if I belt 'im there's a reason for it, like 'is writin' fuck off an' that. 'E's a good speller.

HELENE. What is it you hit Sam with?

ALAN. Just me belt like. I was feelin' bad anyway, yer know, because me money had just run out. Bein' in the hotel, not knowin' what t'do. The kid he likes posh hotels, don't yer, Sam?

SAM *lifts his leg, he lets it fall.*

'E knows 'ow t'live even at 'is age. Then 'e tekks stuff all the time. I was dead worried, I can tell yer, about me money. I knew we couldn't pay the bill like. Yer can't explain that t'the kid. Give us me fag now, son?

SAM (*a moan*).

ALAN. Come on, don't start that again.

SAM (*a moan*).

ALAN. Yer know I'll get angry, don't yer?

HELENE. Give Alan the cigarette, Sam.

SAM *gives* ALAN *the cigarette.*

ALAN. Bloody 'ell.

HELENE. Thank you.

SAM *lifts his leg, he lets it fall. He pushes* ALAN *so that he can lie on him, he lies with his head on* ALAN*'s lap.*

ALAN. Yer must 'ave a magic touch.

ALAN *smokes.*

'Ave yer got kids of yer own?

HELENE. I have two daughters who have grown up now.

ALAN. We 'ad bets about whether you were married. 'E said you weren't, I said you were.

HELENE. No, my husband is in Cologne. He will be coming here for the weekend. At first the business it is mine – my husband he is a lawyer – but as the business grow he join me. Now he do all the business work for our company.

ALAN. Is that 'im who keeps ringing up?

HELENE. Yes.

ALAN. 'Ave yer told 'im about us?

HELENE. Not yet, I have not.

ALAN. We'd better go then, 'adn't we?

HELENE. It is up to you, no?

ALAN. What's he gonna say?

HELENE. He will be a little shocked, I think. He is an upright man.

A slight pause.

ALAN. We'd better go then, a reckon. (*Looking at him:*) Sam?

SAM *has his eyes closed.* HELENE *stands up. She kneels close to* ALAN.

HELENE. It is up to you.

ALAN. I don't understand you, yer know. I mean I know yer dead kind an' that. Why d'yer wanna get yersel' in trouble just for us?

HELENE. I will not be in trouble.

ALAN. If I came 'ere an' found someone like me, I'd fuckin' kill 'em.

HELENE *shrugs. She sits.*

We'd better go like.

HELENE. It is up to you.

ALAN. Yer keep sayin' that.

HELENE. Perhaps if you behave a little more politely, he would like that.

A slight pause.

Perhaps if you do not swear quite so much. He know what a fuck is, we do not talk about it.

ALAN. Fuck, do I swear a lot?

HELENE. I think you do.

ALAN. I'm sorry, like.

A slight pause.

HELENE. Perhaps if you do not hit Sam it would be a good thing also. My husband he like children.

A slight pause.

ALAN. Yeh.

HELENE. That is all the things I mention. It is now up to you?

ALAN. Yeh.

A slight pause.

Can a breathe like, yer know?

HELENE. I think you may breathe if you wish.

ALAN. Ta. Thanks.

A slight pause.

I'm a cunt, aren't I?

HELENE. This is a bad start already.

ALAN. What?

HELENE. That word you say.

ALAN. Oh fuck.

A slight pause.

HELENE. It is hard for you, no?

ALAN. Yeh. It's very hard, like.

HELENE. This is because you do not think about what I say, you just carry on as before.

ALAN. A do think.

HELENE. But, no, I do not think so.

ALAN. A do.

A slight pause.

It's you, yer worse than a bloody officer. At least yer can swear about them and tell them to –

A slight pause.

HELENE. You will have to forgive me, Alan. But it is my house.

ALAN. Yeh, all right.

HELENE. Also I would like my gold ring back from Sam. It is very dear to me, it belong to my father.

ALAN *looks at* SAM.

ALAN. A reckon 'e's asleep. I can get it now.

HELENE. No, not now.

ALAN (*going into* SAM's *pocket*). It's the only way yer'll get it, like.

HELENE (*firmly*). No.

ALAN *stops.*

ALAN. I'm tellin' yer yer'll never get it. You 'aven't seen 'im.

HELENE. Then I will not get it.

ALAN. It's up t'you. Don't blame me.

ALAN *goes into* SAM's *pocket*

HELENE (*firmly*). I have said no, Alan.

ALAN *stops. He stares at her.* HELENE *stares back.*

I do not know what you think of me.

ALAN *backs down.*

ALAN. All right, you win.

HELENE. Thank you.

A slight pause.

ALAN. I am just a cunt, yer know.

HELENE. Do you enjoy being that word?

ALAN. Yer never bloody stop, do you?

HELENE. No.

ALAN. Yeh, I enjoy bein' a cunt. Why not?

HELENE. I think I have to tell you something now. As cunts go you are a very bad cunt. A very poor that word. The marks you would get would be very low.

HELENE *unbuttons and rolls up her sleeve.*

Because I have to tell you, I once knew a cunt. He did things to me you could not imagine.

HELENE *shows him the number tattooed on her arm.*

With him, you are nothing. You are a nobody. You do not even begin.

ALAN *is silent for a moment.*

ALAN. What is it, like?

HELENE. You do not know?

ALAN. No.

A slight pause.

HELENE. I was in the camps, Alan.

ALAN. Sorry like, I don't know much about it.

HELENE. At Birkenau.

A pause.

ALAN. I'm sorry. I don't know what yer want us t'say?

HELENE. I want you to understand you are not that word.

ALAN. You're the one swearin' now.

A slight pause.

I know people went there an' were gassed, yer know.

HELENE. Tell me what it was like to be there?

ALAN thinks.

ALAN. That's all a know really.

HELENE. Please use your imagination. Please.

ALAN thinks.

ALAN. I can't. It must've been like hell.

HELENE. Please, some more.

ALAN. Hell and hell and hell, yer know. I'm sorry.

HELENE. Yes, what else?

ALAN. I mean it wasn't us that did it, was it?

HELENE. No.

ALAN. I mean I know women an' children were starved to death an' that. I've seen pictures of 'em, yer know, the skeletons. I jus' don't see what it's got t'do with me, that's all.

ALAN shrugs.

Honestly, I don't.

HELENE. I cannot tell you, Alan, how a thing like that makes you hate, as you talk about hate. Or what it was like to steal from your neighbour because you have nothing. But your neighbour have nothing, this one thing perhaps, which you steal. Like Sam steal.

ALAN. Yeh.

HELENE buttons her sleeve.

HELENE. He was a soldier. A guard. He was at the station when we arrived. He even helped my mother by not pushing her. I was ten years old.

A slight pause.

He walked beside me through the gates. Then there must have been a mistake because, at the hut we were taken to, we children and women had to get undressed in front of him. He was so embarrassed. I was too. My mother told me not to be silly. Then a female guard arrived and the mistake was put right. But a minute later a message came. I was to get dressed. I had to put on another girl's clothes because, by now, mine were at the bottom of the heap. I so wanted to be clean that I cried. My mother pushed me to the door. She pushed me away. I saw him outside. I have tried to forget his kindness, but somehow it is impossible.

A slight pause.

The next day he came and asked me what I liked to do. I told him painting. I made that up because it was really my brother who was the painter, but at that moment I could not think. He brought me paper from his quarters and some crayons. I had to draw him. He smiled and pulled faces – I had to draw these too. I was hiding my paper from him because of this lie. But I liked him very much. He told me his name was Kurt. He was twenty-four.

A slight pause.

One day he took me to his billet. My sketches were up on the wall by his bunk. It was then he told me I had been lying to him. But I sat down on the stool as usual. And, with a little cane, he flicked at my legs as I drew. He looked so, so angry. I saw my friend Kurt for the first time. I think he wanted me to cry but I could not because, by now, my body was so dried up. We did not have tears. He told me I would pay for what I had done. He had my head shaved again. I had to draw him, on my scalp, with a razor blade.

A slight pause.

When I was better he had my head shaved again. You see what you nearly do to me?

Silence.

ALAN. Yeh, sorry.

A slight pause.

Yer didn't tell us before, like.

A slight pause.

HELENE. Kurt, he take away my faith forever.

A slight pause.

ALAN. Yer gettin' upset, aren't yer?

HELENE. A little.

ALAN. Don't get upset, eh? I couldn't stand that.

A pause.

Yer feelin' better?

HELENE *rubs her hand up and down her leg.*

Yer cold?

HELENE. A little still.

ALAN. It is gettin' a bit cold.

ALAN takes his shoes and socks off, he does it carefully so as not to disturb SAM.

Put my socks on. Go on, they're clean, it's better than nothin'.

HELENE *takes her shoes off. She puts* ALAN's *white socks on.*

Better?

HELENE. Thank you.

ALAN. I know I'm a cunt, I don't mean it, yer know. (*Realising.*) Sorry, that word.

A slight pause.

We ought t'start a swear box.

SAM *changes position. He gets himself more comfortable with his head still on* ALAN's *lap.* ALAN *runs his fingers through* SAM's *hair.*

Don't reckon 'e'll sleep tonight now. 'E never does when 'e sleeps like this. I love 'im, yer know. 'E's the only thing I 'ave. Don't know why I hit him. Easy target, isn't he? Mebbe that's why.

HELENE *looks up at* ALAN.

Like yer say, I don't ever listen to anything anyone ever sez. I never 'ave. Why should I? They don't listen to me.

A slight pause.

Yer say I should do this, yer say I should do that. I don't want to. I know yer see me as a kind of conquest like. It's just I hate the fuckin' bastards. Alwez 'ave. Everyone. Alwez will. It's the way I want it.

A slight pause.

I mean you're just a cunt like everyone else. Bit less, mebbe. Sorry, like. Yer still out for what yer can get – only yer want it from me. I can't give it yer, like. Sorry.

A slight pause.

It's why me an' 'im 'ad better go.

ALAN *takes his jumper off. He is wearing a crucifix on a chain round his neck. He gives the jumper to* HELENE.

HELENE. Thank you.

HELENE *puts the jumper on.*

Before you go, I would like my ring back please. All my family died. My father he gave me his ring. I spent my life there hiding it, I should have it back.

ALAN *delves into* SAM'*s pockets. He finds the ring. He gives it to* HELENE. HELENE *puts the ring on her finger.*

Thank you.

ALAN. D'you want the other stuff?

HELENE. No, he may keep the other items.

ALAN *takes the crucifix from round his neck.*

ALAN. See this? This is mine. I took it from a soldier. An Argie, like. A keepsake, yer know.

He gives it to HELENE. HELENE *looks.*

The bastard was dead when a took it.

HELENE. You?

ALAN (*shrugging*). It was too dark, yer know. I alwez think it might 'ave been me.

HELENE. You do not mind?

ALAN. It's me job, isn't it. I'll 'ave it back, thanks.

HELENE *gives it to him,* ALAN *puts the crucifix round his neck.*

ALAN. I'll let him sleep a bit, eh?

HELENE. Yes.

ALAN. 'E don't sleep well. It's 'cos we're kind o'scared, an' yet we're not. Yer have this thing in yer body called adrenaline that takes over. It gets t'the point where yer'll do owt. The officers punch it out of yer, punch yer forward. It's a great feeling. Yer body is like runnin' on its own – a bit like it's not really you, but somebody else. It's this somebody else who's doin' what yer have t'do. Like kill. It isn't you at all. The officers say that's the way yer mind copes wi' being scared. I reckon it's a bit more than that, like – I reckon it's the way yer cope wi' killin' people, it not bein' you doin' it, if you understand me. That's 'ow a get wi' the nipper – jus' mad, jus' someone else. Yer know what me real fear is? That one day I might kill 'im by mistake. I keep this crucifix, 'cos I remember what that Argie looked like. 'E wasn't damaged, yer know, 'e was just dead. I see the nipper like that sometimes. It's why I always apologise to 'im. I make mesel' apologise. If I didn't mekk mesel' apologise, I'd just go on, yer know. Then what would 'appen? He'd be dead. Yer see 'ow scared of meself I am? Scared of what I might do? I've been thinkin' a lot about this lately. Me bein' on me own wi' the nipper, yer know. I can't work it out – can't work mesel' out really. A just reckon we hurt each other because we both enjoy it. It's odd t'say that about a kid, isn't it? But kids know, yer know, I've learnt that. I've jus' been reckonin' that I 'ave to be the adult one of us. A bit like you said. I've been thinkin' that to be adult I ought to be a bit firmer with him – even stop all the apologising, mebbe. Then I just worry about what a said before. Yer see me problem? It all boils down to the fact that I 'ave a terrible temper. Someone has to help me control it. I'd like Sam to, but 'e's just a kid. That's why a need you to help me. How do a stop mesel' from enjoying hurtin' people? If I knew that, like, I'd be all right. Then mebbe Sam'd learn that from me an' we'd be better together. 'E's gettin' worse. I know it's my fault. 'E used to have a few words 'e said – only a few like – but now he sez nowt, as yer've seen. 'E's just gone right back. 'E's mekkin' me madder all the time, 'cos I'm gettin' nowhere with 'im. I'm apologising an' apologising. Yer saw his back, I was close then. I know I'm that word, but I'd like your help with 'im, please. If yer don't do it for me, do it for the nipper. None of this is his fault. Will yer help me with Sam?

HELENE. Which words did he speak?

ALAN. He did say please and thank you like. I was meant t'do what they call reinforce it. Or 'is mother was, before she fucked off. I mean I blame 'er for all this. If 'e could just get back to what 'e was, then I'd be better. I know that's thinkin' of me – but it's thinkin' of 'im an' all. Tony used to be great with the kid. Tony's my mate. He was a corporal, now he's a sergeant. Not the sergeant who ran off with my wife – he's a different bastard altogether. Tony's great. He's the one told me I should go f' lance-corporal. He told me I should be more ambitious. I 'ave it in me, I know that. We've fell out a bit recently. Tony's the one told me that Sheila was a cunt. I just floored him. I know I shouldn't have done. But if yer love someone, that's the way, isn't it? I feel sorry f' Tony, now 'e won't speak, I reckon 'e should get over it, yer know, but 'e won't. I reckon it's daft to carry on bearin' grudges. I don't bear 'im one – 'e was right. I broke the poor bastard's jaw. 'E didn't report me, 'e could 'ave done. That's one thing in 'is favour. Tony an' me we've

alwez been on the same tours, like 'ere in Germany. He
likes his life now, with his kids an' his promotion. Don't
blame 'im. It's just sad t'think yer can't keep yer best mate.
He's in married quarters now. We 'ad a married quarter
before Sheila fucked off. I went back into barracks. I 'ad
to. The' wanted the nipper fostered in England. I were
fostered – it's a pile of shit. The Families Officer is shit.
They're all shit. The' wouldn't 'ave it I could look after
'im. I know I could if I 'ad the chance. He needs a mother.
I want to get married again. I were in home after home,
yer know. I can see the nipper going my way. It depresses
me, I can tell yer.

SAM *changes position, he gets himself more comfortable on*
ALAN*'s lap.*

I 'ad three months. That was four months ago.

SAM *wakes with a start, he sits up and opens his eyes.*

Yer've bin asleep, son.

SAM *squats on his haunches.*

Yer bin dreamin'?

SAM *nods.*

Nightmares?

SAM *shakes his head.*

What about?

SAM *takes his felt-tip pen from his sock and writes on his*
arm. ALAN *watches.*

'E's put huntin' deer, forests. 'E must've been dreamin'
about that.

SAM *clips his felt-tip pen back into his sock.* ALAN *stands*
up.

We're goyn t'go, Sam. We've got t'go.

SAM *sees the ring on* HELENE*'s finger. He points*
furiously.

SAM (*an ear-piercing shriek*).

SAM *looks at* ALAN. ALAN *squats down.*

ALAN. It's her ring, son. She wanted it.

SAM (*an ear-piercing shriek*).

ALAN. It's the lady's, son. It belongs to her.

SAM (*an ear-piercing shriek*).

HELENE. If Sam scream once more in that spoilt way I will take back all my other items.

SAM *takes the other things from his pocket, he throws them at her. He curls up into a ball, his head on* ALAN'*s leg. He sucks his thumb.*

ALAN. A reckon it's the ring 'e wanted.

A slight pause.

HELENE. Is it the ring you want, Sam?

SAM *is silent.*

ALAN. Yeh, it is, a know.

SAM *stretches out and raises his leg. He clumps it down angrily.*

I told yer the kid wasn't daft.

HELENE. Then, Sam, we will do a deal. We will put the items together and we will pick.

SAM *moves quickly, he kneels on his haunches. He goes to grab them.* HELENE *covers the things with her hands.*

Ah. Ah.

SAM *stops.*

But I will pick first.

SAM *violently shakes his head. He goes to grab them again.* HELENE *pushes his hands away.*

No, Sam.

SAM *slaps her hard across the face.* HELENE *moves her head back slightly, but the blow still catches her.*

I will not be attacked either, Sam.

SAM *curls up into a ball, his head on* ALAN's *leg.*

ALAN. Yer've done it now, like.

HELENE. I think he is the one who hurt me.

A slight pause.

Sam?

SAM is *violently sucking at his thumb. He is rocking.*

Sam? I tell you what we will do, Sam. You may pick first, but –

SAM *moves quickly, he kneels on his haunches.*

Ah. Ah.

HELENE *covers the things with her hands.*

But we will both say thank you for what we pick.

SAM *nods.*

Not a thank you like that, but a proper thank you. Like this: thank you.

SAM *takes his felt-tip pen from his sock.*

No, not a written thank you.

SAM *throws the felt-tip pen at her.*

That is my deal. That is what I am offering you.

SAM *looks imploringly towards* ALAN. *He is bobbing up and down.*

SAM (*a loud shriek*).

ALAN. It's up t'you, son.

SAM *looks at* HELENE. HELENE *takes the ring from her finger, she puts it with the other things.* SAM *makes a grab for it.* HELENE *picks the ring up.*

HELENE. Ah. Ah. Sam is a good boy to keep his promise, no? He must say thank you.

SAM *nods.*

Sam is making a promise, no?

SAM *nods.*

Good, then I will trust him.

HELENE *puts the ring with the other things.* SAM *starts to make a grab.*

Ah. Ah.

SAM *stops.*

Now Sam may.

SAM *is still. He slowly picks up the ring.*

I take the teaspoon.

HELENE *picks it up.*

Now we both say thank you.

SAM *curls up into a ball, his head on* ALAN*'s leg.*

ALAN. I could 'ave told you 'e wouldn't.

HELENE. But he must say thank you, no? He made a promise.

ALAN. Say thank you, son.

SAM *is silent.*

HELENE *stands up.*

HELENE. But, yes, he must, this minute. Otherwise I take it back.

SAM *goes tighter into the ball. He rocks.*

ALAN. Yer won't get it.

HELENE. But, yes, I think so, no.

SAM *puts the ring into his trouser pocket, he holds both his hands over it.*

HELENE *goes to* SAM, *she stands over him.*

This is not the way for a boy to behave.

HELENE *bends down.*

SAM *goes tighter into the ball.*

HELENE *takes hold of* SAM*'s legs and pulls him away from* ALAN. SAM *tries to remain in the ball as he is pulled along. He begins to kick out with his legs.* HELENE *stops.* SAM *squats on his haunches, his thumb in his mouth.*

Which way is it to be, Sam?

SAM is *silent.* ALAN *stands up.*

ALAN. D'yer want me to get it?

SAM (*a shriek*).

HELENE. No. Sam may keep it, but he is going to say thank you. We will wait.

A slight pause.

SAM (*a quieter shriek*).

HELENE. This is nowhere near good enough. He is not even trying.

SAM (*a series of little shrieks*).

HELENE. Terrible, terrible.

SAM (*an ear-piercing shriek*).

HELENE. We are going to be here a long time, no?

A slight pause.

HELENE *kneels down by* SAM.

It is not very much I ask of you, Sam. This one little thing. Please do it for me.

SAM *moves quickly, he kneels in front of* HELENE. *He slaps her hard across the face. It happens so quickly that* HELENE *hardly sees it coming. She is visibly shaken,* SAM *has really hurt her.*

A slight pause.

No, Sam.

SAM *slaps her again with all the strength he can find.*

A slight pause.

HELENE *shakes her head.*

No, Sam.

SAM (*an ear-piercing shriek*).

HELENE. The word is thank you.

SAM *slaps* HELENE. HELENE *flinches, she is really being hurt.*

A slight pause.

HELENE *shakes her head.*

No, Sam.

SAM *slaps* HELENE.

But you know you can hurt me, so why?

SAM *takes the ring from his trouser pocket, he throws it at her. He scuttles across the ground towards* ALAN. *He curls up into the ball at* ALAN's *feet. He rocks.*

HELENE *picks up the ring.*

A short silence.

ALAN. Yer've got what yer wanted, 'aven't yer.

A short silence.

HELENE *stands up. She goes to* SAM *and takes hold of his legs. She pulls him away from* ALAN. SAM *begins to kick out in all directions.*

HELENE. Stand up.

SAM (*an ear-piercing shriek*).

HELENE. You are going to stand up.

*HELENE tries to start to lift SAM to his feet. SAM kicks
out and struggles.*

No, Sam.

*It takes a while but eventually HELENE gets SAM
standing.*

SAM looks imploringly at ALAN.

SAM (*a loud shriek*).

ALAN. It's nothing t'do with me, son.

SAM (*a loud shriek*).

SAM stamps his foot. After a few moments he stops.

HELENE puts the ring into SAM's trouser pocket.

HELENE. Thank you.

SAM takes the ring out and throws it to the ground.

HELENE picks it up.

SAM, defiantly, puts both his hands in his trouser pockets.

HELENE takes hold of SAM.

SAM (*an ear-piercing shriek*).

*It takes a while but eventually HELENE manages to get one
of SAM's hands from one of his pockets. SAM is struggling
all the time. HELENE puts the ring into the pocket. SAM
tries to get his hand back in to take it out. HELENE is
determined to stop him, she keeps her hand over the pocket.
It is a real battle.*

SAM (*an ear-piercing shriek*).

HELENE. No, that is not it.

*It takes a while but eventually SAM stops fighting. The ring
is still in his pocket. They are still. HELENE keeps tight
hold of him.*

What must you say now'

SAM (*a shriek*).

HELENE. No, this is not good enough.

SAM (*a different shriek*).

HELENE. No.

> SAM *tries to struggle free.* HELENE *keeps tight hold.* HELENE *wins, they are still.*

SAM (*a moan*).

HELENE. No.

> *A short silence.*

This is right, you have a think about it.

SAM (*a shriek*).

HELENE. No.

> *A short silence.*

SAM (*a shriek*).

HELENE. If you wish to play this game we will be here a long time.

> SAM *tries to struggle free.* HELENE *keeps tight hold, she wins. They are still again.*

Now we have these words I think.

> *A slight pause.*

SAM (*barely discernible*). Thank you.

HELENE. It is better, but not good enough.

SAM (*a shriek*).

> *A short silence.*

HELENE. Yes, you have another think.

> *A short silence.*

SAM (*more discernible*). Thank you.

HELENE. No.

SAM (*more discernible still*). Thank you.

HELENE. No.

SAM (*clearer*). Thank you.

ALAN *is looking in disbelief.*

ALAN. That's about as good as 'e ever was.

HELENE. I cannot tell what he say yet.

SAM (*clearer still, but it is obvious* SAM *cannot speak very well, even when he tries*). Thank you.

HELENE. No.

SAM (*beginning to try*). Thank you.

HELENE. Better.

SAM (*really trying*). Thank you.

HELENE. Come on, Sam.

SAM (*really concentrating*). Thank you.

HELENE. And again, please.

SAM (*really quite clearly*). Thank you very much.

HELENE. What?

SAM. Thank you very much.

HELENE. Good. Better.

HELENE *releases her grip.* SAM *starts to run on the spot.*

ALAN. D'yer want t'wee, son?

SAM *nods.*

Well do it then.

SAM *starts to undo his trousers.*

Not 'ere, not in front of us. Go somewhere else.

SAM *exits quickly.*

A short silence.

HELENE. You see, it is easy.

A short silence.

SAM *returns, he stops. He takes the ring from his pocket and throws it at her.*

ALAN. A reckon 'e's changed 'is mind.

HELENE *picks up the ring, she stands up and looks at* SAM.

SAM *looks imploringly at* ALAN.

SAM (*a loud shriek*).

ALAN. It's nowt t'do wi' me, son. Not now.

HELENE *goes to* SAM.

SAM (*an ear-piercing shriek*).

HELENE *holds him. She puts the ring back into his pocket without much difficulty.*

SAM (*a shriek*).

ALAN. Yer'd better do as the lady tells yer.

SAM *drops to the ground. He curls up into a tight ball.* HELENE *looks at* SAM. SAM *is rocking.*

Leave 'im be, like.

SAM (*a grunt of agreement*).

HELENE *goes to the other things from* SAM's *pocket which are still on the ground, she picks them up.*

HELENE. Right, Sam, it is your turn to pick again.

SAM (*a shriek*).

HELENE. I have enough of these noises.

HELENE *goes to* SAM *and kneels down. She spreads the things in front of her. She picks up the teaspoon.*

I take the teaspoon. Thank you. Your turn.

SAM *is silent.*

HELENE *picks up the badge.*

This little blue badge, who is this? This is not mine.

SAM *moves quickly, he kneels. He tries to slap* HELENE. HELENE *is ready this time and her hand goes up and stops him.* SAM *quickly returns to the ball.*

ALAN. His mother gave it to 'im.

HELENE. Sam miss a go. This is mine, I keep it.

SAM (*an ear-piercing shriek*).

HELENE. No, it is mine now.

SAM (*an ear-piercing shriek*).

HELENE. If Sam want it, he have to ask for it, and say please.

SAM (*a shriek*).

HELENE. No, that is not please.

A short silence.

HELENE *stands up with the teaspoon and badge in her hand.*

Good, it is mine.

HELENE *goes to* ALAN.

It is a lovely little badge, no? It is beautiful, I think.

ALAN. Give it 'im, eh?

HELENE. No, why should I?

ALAN. It's 'is, yer know.

HELENE. But we make a deal.

ALAN. 'E's just a kid, can't yer see?

SAM*'s hand comes out of the ball, he picks up the other things which are still on the ground and stuffs them back into his trouser pockets.*

Give 'im it, please.

HELENE. No.

ALAN. Look, I'm not jokin' yer know.

HELENE. I do not joke either, Alan.

A slight pause.

ALAN. Just give 'im it, now, will yer.

HELENE. No.

ALAN (*with real, quiet aggression*). Just fuckin' well give it
 'im before a nut yer.

HELENE. No.

   ALAN *grabs* HELENE*'s hand. He twists it.*

   You are hurting me.

   HELENE *drops the badge.* ALAN *picks it up, he throws it
   to* SAM.

   SAM *scrambles for it. He puts the badge in his trouser
   pocket. He returns to the ball. He rocks.*

ALAN. You're a fuckin' nutta, you. Treatin' a kid like that.

HELENE. No.

ALAN. Yer fuckin' warped.

HELENE. No.

ALAN. Yer think yer so good, don't yer?

HELENE. No.

ALAN. Yer a fuckin' nutta, I'm tellin' yer. You think I couldn't
 do that?

HELENE. Yes.

ALAN. Yer ought t'be locked up. Fuck you.

Scene Two

The wood that evening. The easel and the painting things have been taken back to the house.

A bright moonlight is shining through the dense growths of pine trees.

ALAN is standing alone. He is wearing his socks and shoes and his jumper.

A pause.

HELENE enters. She is wearing a coat which is open, and she is smoking a cigarette.

ALAN does not see her.

A slight pause.

HELENE. Sam, he is in bed, no?

  ALAN turns.

ALAN. Yeh. He was crying. I've not seen 'im cry before. Normally 'e's a tough little basket.

HELENE. Perhaps I was a little harsh.

ALAN. A little? Yer must be jokin'.

HELENE. I think it is his pride which is hurt, no?

  A slight pause.

  On Friday, when my husband arrive, I must ask you not to swear as we prepare for the Sabbath.

ALAN. What's that like?

HELENE. On Saturday we give our thank you's to God.

ALAN. Dyer want us to?

  HELENE smiles.

HELENE. Not unless you wish. I ask you only to respect my belief.

ALAN. Yeh. (*Realising.*) Course you must be Jewish, aren't yer?

HELENE. A little. A little. But not so little I do not keep the Sabbath. It is something I must do.

ALAN. Is your husband?

HELENE. Yes.

ALAN. Yer miss a lot of history when yer young, don't yer? I've been standin' ere thinkin' that.

HELENE *takes a step towards him.*

HELENE. It was my faith in God, Alan, which kept me strong. Which is not to say that is for you. For all of us it must be different. God, he is us, I think. I try to keep Him good, in my little way. God, he is as forgiving as we are. I think, now, you must learn to forgive.

ALAN. Yer off again, aren't yer?

HELENE. But, of course.

ALAN. What do I do then?

HELENE. That is not for me to say. I ask you to forgive, a little, that is all.

ALAN. Who?

HELENE. Me, for bullying you. I ask you to understand the risk I take, standing here with you, saying the things I do. You still think it is easy for me?

ALAN. Yeh.

HELENE. It is not. It is the hardest thing I do.

ALAN *shrugs.*

ALAN. Why?

HELENE. Because I risk myself. You must risk.

ALAN. Risk what like?

HELENE. Risk being wrong. Risk being hurt. This is what forgiveness is.

ALAN *thinks for a moment.*

ALAN. Yer too good f' me, like. Can I 'ave a drag of yer fag?

> HELENE *gives him the cigarette.* ALAN *takes a couple of deep puffs. He gives her it back.*

Ta. Yer just mekk us feel bad all the time.

HELENE. This is what I try to do.

ALAN. I 'aven't changed me mind, yer know. Yer just a cunt. Yer won't get us t'change me mind.

> HELENE *shrugs.*

HELENE. It is up to you.

ALAN. Why say that?

HELENE. It is the truth.

> ALAN *thinks for a moment.*

ALAN. No, yer just a cunt.

> HELENE *turns and starts to walk to the house.*

> ALAN *calls after her.*

Yer'll 'ave to apologise to the nipper an' all.

HELENE. I will not.

> HELENE *stops and turns.*

I will apologise to him, if you will apologise to me.

ALAN. Yer must be jokin'.

> HELENE *turns to go back to the house.*

Don't go like. A need yer.

> HELENE *turns back to* ALAN.

HELENE. I will take that as the apology. It would be wrong for me to apologise to Sam.

ALAN. You are a cunt, though.

HELENE. This become a game now, I think?

ALAN. Can I 'ave a drag of your fag?

HELENE *goes to* ALAN, *she gives him the cigarette.*
ALAN *takes two deep puffs.*

Can I keep it?

HELENE *thinks for a moment.*

HELENE. Yes, if you wish.

ALAN *moves quite slowly to stub the cigarette out on the back of his hand.* HELENE *knocks the cigarette away.*

No.

Silence.

HELENE *bends down and stubs out the cigarette.*

ALAN. Yer have t'see what things are like, don't yer?

SAM *enters. He stops. He is wearing pyjamas.*

Couldn't yer sleep, kid?

SAM *shakes his head.*

Never mind, eh.

SAM *watches* HELENE. *He walks to* ALAN *keeping as much distance as possible between himself and her, skirting right round.*

We'll go t'sleep, 'ere, eh? We'll forget that horrible woman.

SAM *sits down. He looks up at* ALAN. ALAN *sits down.* SAM *sits between* ALAN's *legs.*

HELENE *remains standing.*

Silence.

HELENE *sits down beside them.*

Silence.

ALAN *takes a packet of cigarettes from his pocket. He offers them to* HELENE.

Want one?

HELENE. No thank you.

ALAN *lights a cigarette. He returns the packet to his pocket. He smokes.*

Silence.

ALAN. Yer don't 'ave t'worry, I won't touch 'im. Yer've got that far.

SAM *holds up his hand with two fingers outstretched.* ALAN *gives him the cigarette.* SAM *smokes.*

Yer tired?

SAM *lifts his leg, he lets it fall.*

HELENE. What are you going to do, Alan?

ALAN. Try an' do as you say, I suppose.

A slight pause.

HELENE. With Sam?

ALAN. D'know like. Just hope, yer know.

HELENE. Hope for what?

ALAN. D'know. Some good to come from it.

HELENE. Come from what?

ALAN. D'know. Me, I suppose. Ask 'im to give me me fag, will yer?

HELENE. Give Alan the cigarette, Sam.

SAM *gives* ALAN *the cigarette.* ALAN *smokes.*

Is there much hope of this?

ALAN. D'know. Mebbe. If I try like.

HELENE. Are you going to try?

ALAN. D'know. Way I feel at the moment, I might.

SAM *kneels. He looks at* HELENE.

HELENE. Would you like to come to me, Sam?

SAM *nods. He goes to* HELENE, *he sits beside her.*

ALAN. Told yer the little bastard was forgiving.

SAM *settles down. He gets himself more comfortable.*

He's a funny kid, one minute this, next minute that. Like me, I suppose.

SAM *takes the gold ring from his trouser pocket in his pyjamas. He plays with it between his fingers.*

HELENE. This moment you feel. How long is this moment going to last?

ALAN. D'know.

HELENE. Please put the cigarette out.

ALAN. Don't you trust me?

HELENE. No.

ALAN *stubs the cigarette out.*

ALAN. Don't know why a did it. Just felt like it.

HELENE. Have you done that before?

ALAN. No.

HELENE. Were you going to do it?

ALAN. Yeh, a was. Hurt mesel' mebbe – is that the reason?

A slight pause.

Hurt mesel' instead of the kid. Prove I'm not a coward – is that the reason?

HELENE. Are you a coward?

ALAN. Yeh. Suppose I must be a bit of a coward, like.

SAM *takes* HELENE's *hand, he starts to play with it.*

ALAN *is thinking.*

I mean if I wasn't me, I'd think only a coward could do what I've done to that kid. If yer get what a mean?

A slight pause.

I don't trust me. You don't trust me. The only person who does trust me is the kid. Odd, isn't it?

A slight pause.

Is that why I've let 'im down, d'yer reckon?

SAM *kneels. He holds up* HELENE's *hand. He looks at her. He shows her her own finger.*

SAM (*clearly with a diminutive little voice*). This finger?

HELENE. Which is the finger you took it from?

SAM. This one.

ALAN *looks in disbelief.* SAM *looks at* ALAN. *He giggles at the sound of his own voice. He puts the ring on* HELENE's *finger. He looks up at her.*

Back later?

HELENE. Yes, you can have it back later.

The three of them are still.

The End.